GEORGE GERSHWIN'S
RHAPSODY IN BLUE
FOR PIANO DUET

INTERMEDIATE
TO ADVANCED

ADAPTED BY
BRENT EDSTROM

ISBN 978-1-4803-7134-7

Visit Hal Leonard Online at
www.halleonard.com

World headquarters, contact:
Hal Leonard
7777 West Bluemound Road
Milwaukee, WI 53213
Email: info@halleonard.com

In Europe, contact:
Hal Leonard Europe Limited
42 Wigmore Street
Marylebone, London, W1U 2RY
Email: info@halleonardeurope.com

In Australia, contact:
Hal Leonard Australia Pty. Ltd.
4 Lentara Court
Cheltenham, Victoria, 3192 Australia
Email: info@halleonard.com.au

INTRODUCTION

Since its premiere at the behest of Paul Whiteman in 1924, George Gershwin's *Rhapsody in Blue* has maintained a unique place in the canon of American symphonic repertoire. As composers versed in the traditions of Western European art music continued to explore the boundaries of tonality, Gershwin's incorporation of jazz and blues elements set the stage for a concert work that received both critical acclaim and broad appeal. Although initially scored for piano and jazz orchestra, the numerous arrangements and orchestrations of the piece speak to the clarity of Gershwin's compositional voice and the popularity of the work. To quote Deems Taylor, a composer and critic who attended the premiere, the piece "hinted at something new, something that had not hitherto been said in music."

Nearly 100 years after the inception of the original composition, this arrangement of *Rhapsody in Blue* represents another interpretation of the venerable work. A goal of the arrangement was to be true to Gershwin's compositional voice while reinterpreting the work for one piano, four hands. It is my sincere hope that the arrangement will be enjoyable to play and will maintain the spirit and integrity of the original composition.

–Brent Edstrom

RHAPSODY IN BLUE

GEORGE GERSHWIN
Adapted by Brent Edstrom

ABOUT THE ARRANGER

Brent Edstrom has published more than 60 books for Hal Leonard's *Jazz Piano Solos* series as well as numerous transcriptions of historically significant jazz pianists. An active composer and scholar, he has received composition commissions from numerous organizations including University of Nebraska and Washington State Music Teachers Association, and he's published a book on the musical application of microcontroller technology for Oxford University Press. His *Concerto for Jazz Piano and Orchestra* has been performed in Europe and the United States, and he himself premiered his *Prairie Songs: Remembering Ántonia*, a song cycle for voice, violin, and piano, based on the novels and letters of Willa Cather.

Also Arranged by Brent Edstrom

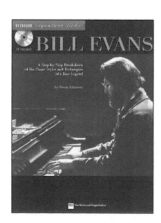

Bill Evans – A Step-by-Step Breakdown of the Piano Styles and Techniques of a Jazz Legend
HL00695714

Bob Marley for Piano Duet
HL00129926

Duke Ellington
HL 00311787